The Long Road to Change

An American Story of Civil Rights and
Barack Obama's Journey to the White House

Rachael Law Schuetz

By Rachael Law Schuetz

Graphic Design Layout by
Rachael Law Schuetz, Louie & Marianne Law

Dedicated to my family,

Thank you for your unique contributions that helped make this, and many dreams a reality.

Grandma Martha and Papa Ralph, thank you for always encouraging me to "go for it, fireball!".

Mom and Dad you are the best parents a girl could have. You've given me strong roots and wings. Thank you for your love, enthusiasm, ideas, and hours of photoshop artwork.

To Nick, my incredible husband, thank you for your love, support, and belief in me. Thanks for the nights of brainstorming and editing!

I can't express how much you all mean to me.
With my love, Rachael

©2009 Rachael Law Schuetz, NRS Enterprises, All Rights Reserved.
No part of this book may be reproduced or transmitted in any form or by any means whatsoever without express written permission from the author, except in the case of brief quotations embodied in critical articles and reviews. Please refer all pertinent questions to the author.

International Standard Book Number (ISBN): 978-0-615-27983-1
Library of Congress Card Catalog Number: 2009901918
Made in the United States of America
Graphic Design ©2009 Rachael Law Schuetz, Louie & Marianne Law of Elegant Images Photography

Photo Credits: All effort has been made in good faith to confirm correct use and citation of images.
Purchased Royalty-Free Big Stock Photos:
4431023 (pg. 5), 4357629 (pg. 6-7), 663043 and 1437265 (pg. 10), 2253791 (pg.12-13), 2953154 (pg. 25), 3815808 (pg. 26), 3929527 (pg. 27), 4115771, 3850865, 3924105, 4359726 (pg. 28), 1093071, 4431010 (pg. 34-35)
Courtesy of the Library of Congress, Prints & Photographs Division:
LC-U9-11696-9A (pg. 1, 3, & 19), LC-USZ62-15887 (pg.11), LC-USZ62-7816 (pg. 11), LC-DIG-ppmsca-19241 (pg. 15), LC-USF33-001112-M1 (pg. 16), LC-DIG-ppmsca-08102 (pg. 17), LC-U9-10363-5 (pg. 18), LC-USZ62-109426 (pg. 20) LC-USW3-038017-E (pg. 21), LC-U9-10364-37 (pg. 22), LC-U9-18985-18A (pg. 23), LC-U9-183B-20 (pg. 23) LC-USZ62-126559 (pg. 30). Public domain pictures from governmental website: Barack Obama (Cover. pg. 1, 3, 4, 24)
6 public domain, royalty-free images, courtesy of www.defenseimagery.mil:
090118-N-4794M-315 Date: 1/18/09, Photographer: YN1 Donna Lou Morgan (C, pg. 1 & 3).
090120-F-6184M-292 Date: 1/20/09, Photographer: SMSgt Thomas Meneguin (Pg. 8-9).
090118-N-1928O-128 Date: 1/18/09, Photographer: MC1 Mark O'Donald (pg. 29).
090120-F-9629D-088 Date: 1/20/09, Photographer: TSgt Suzanne M. Day (pg. 31).
090120-F-3961R-919 Date: 1/20/09, Photographer: MSgt Cecillo Ricardo &
090120-N-0106C-345 Date: 1/20/09, Photographer: MC1 Daniel J. Calderon (pg. 32, 33).

All correspondence should be addressed to:
Rachael Law Schuetz
NRS Enterprises
P.O. Box 1638
Bend, Oregon 97709
rachael.schuetz@mac.com

www.longroadtochange.com

The Long Road to Change

An American Story of Civil Rights and
Barack Obama's Journey to the White House

By Rachael Law Schuetz

Graphic Design Layout by
Rachael Law Schuetz, Louie & Marianne Law

January 20, 2009, the day Barack Obama became President, is a day that we will always remember. All of America stopped and watched history in the making.

It was a cold, winter morning in Washington D.C., but the two million Americans who gathered to watch this event looked anything but cold. We could see the hope and pride warming their hearts. We heard songs of peace and words of courage. We saw people unified by a common dream.

The crowd stretched two miles long. People filled the streets from the Capitol Building to the Lincoln Memorial, waiting to see Barack Obama become the first African American President. Some people had waited their whole lives for a moment like this.

America had been waiting for this moment much longer. Our story begins long before January 20, 2009, and even long before Barack Obama was born.

Over 400 years ago, people from England traveled to America to build a new home. The English colonists brought people from Africa to be their slaves. The slaves were forced to work long days, with no pay, and were treated very badly. Slavery was a terrible thing.

Slavery was allowed in the United States for almost 250 years. There were many strong Americans called Abolitionists, who declared that slavery was wrong. Their speeches, meetings, and books spoke against slavery with words like freedom and change.

Frederick Douglass and Harriet Tubman, Abolitionsits

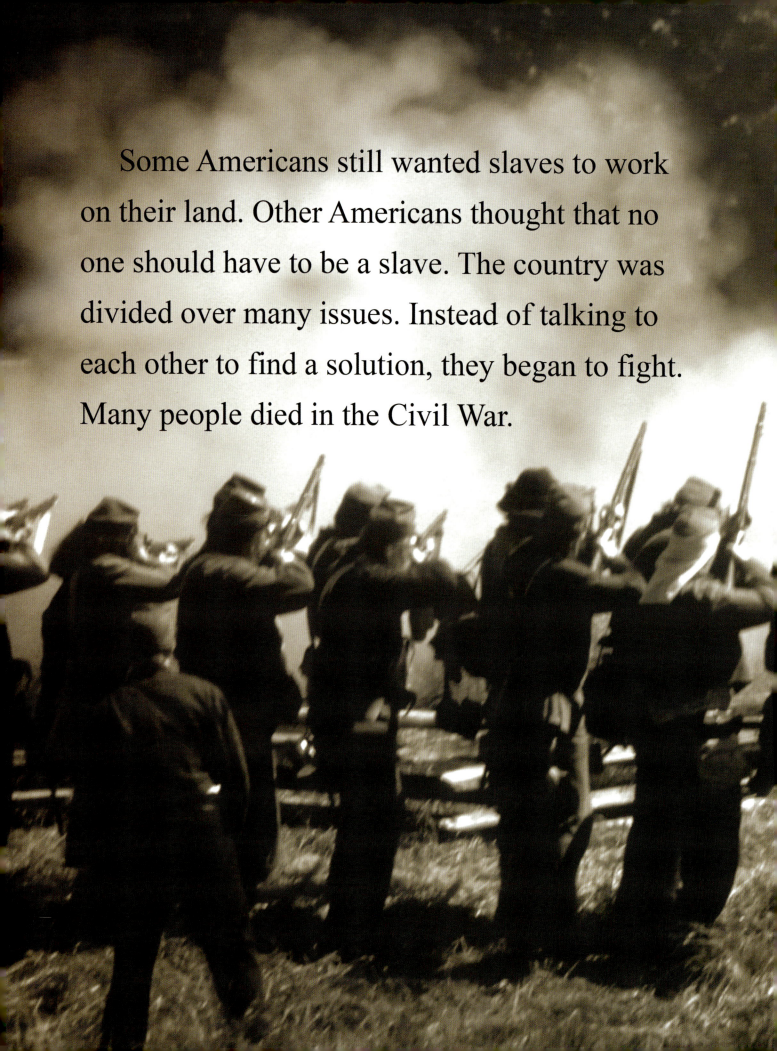

Some Americans still wanted slaves to work on their land. Other Americans thought that no one should have to be a slave. The country was divided over many issues. Instead of talking to each other to find a solution, they began to fight. Many people died in the Civil War.

President Abraham Lincoln had the wisdom and compassion to know that this treatment of African Americans was wrong. In 1863 he wrote a law called the Emancipation Proclamation that ended most slavery. Two years later, the Civil War was over and all slavery in America was declared illegal.

President Lincoln and other Abolitonists had made the first big step, but there was still a long road ahead before African Americans were treated equally.

Although it had been 100 years since the Civil War, there was still hate in the United States. African Americans were not given the same rights as white Americans. Black children could not go to school with white children. There were signs on restaurants, buses, and water fountains that said WHITE ONLY or COLORED ONLY.

This treatment, called segregation, was cruel and unfair. People began to stand up to these unfair laws by marching for freedom. Soon, thousands more joined in.

Dr. Martin Luther King Jr. was a strong American who stood up for equal rights. Instead of violence, he used speeches about love and equality to fight racism. Dr. Martin Luther King Jr. hoped his own children would one day live in a world where they were treated equally. He dreamed of a peaceful world, where anyone could succeed.

Dr. King was doing wonderful things for our country, but not everyone agreed with him. One terrible day he was shot and killed. Dr. Martin Luther King Jr. had given his life to improving the lives of others. Sadly, there was a long road ahead for his dreams of change.

In 1955, an African American woman named Rosa Parks had the courage to say no to segregation. While on a city bus, Mrs. Parks was told to get out of her seat because a white man wanted to sit down. She said "no". Any person, of any color, should be able to sit on the bus.

Rosa Parks with Dr. Martin Luther King Jr.

Many Americans agreed with Rosa Parks. They decided to stop riding the city buses until these unfair laws were changed. 381 days later a law was passed declaring segregation of buses to be illegal. Rosa Parks made important, courageous steps down the long road to change.

Because of Abraham Lincoln, Dr. Martin Luther King Jr., Rosa Parks, and so many other Americans, things slowly began to change.

People stood up for their freedom through speeches, books, and peaceful marches.

There were more laws written, taking down the WHITE ONLY and COLORED ONLY signs.

Kids could go to school together and people could sit together. The healing had begun, but there was still a very long road ahead.

On August 4, 1961, about two years before Dr. King's speeches, Barack Obama was born. Barack's mother was a white American. Barack's father was Black and grew up in Kenya, a country in Africa.

In the fifth grade, Barack went to school in Hawaii. At his school there were only three African American students. Barack was sometimes treated badly and he experienced the challenges of racism. Even though it wasn't always easy, he worked hard in school and was a very good student.

Barack Obama went to college to learn more about helping the United States. After graduating, he worked in his community to make sure people had the things they needed like jobs, food, and a safe place to live. Barack met his wife Michelle and together they continued to find ways to help other Americans.

Barack Obama believed in the strength of America, and he helped others believe too. In 2004, the people of Illinois voted for Obama to be their senator. As a senator he worked in our government to carry out his dreams for the United States. After three years, Barack Obama was nominated to run for President of the United States of America.

Obama inspired millions of people with his ideas and work. Young people, old people, black people, white people, people of different religions, colors, and states worked together. Along with Obama, they all believed that they could make America a better place.

On November 4, 2008, Barack Obama won the election for President of the United States of America! People all over the world rejoiced. America had elected its first African American President. President Obama had inspired people to have faith in America and in themselves.

The day before President Obama's inauguration, America celebrated Dr. Martin Luther King Jr. Day. We stopped to remember how Dr. King made the world a better place. It hurt to learn about things like slavery and prejudice. But we were proud that Dr. Martin Luther King Jr. used his words of love and peace to heal a country sick from hate.

America was not at the end of its journey, but change had come. The very next day, an African American would be the President of the United States.

On, January 20th, 2009, Barack Obama became the first African American man to become President of the United States. Fifty years ago, people might not have believed such a thing could be possible. Watching President Obama speak made us feel like we could do anything with our lives. He made us feel like there are no limits to what we can become. He made us feel that even a small act of goodness, could help change the world.

"This is the meaning of our liberty and our creed — why men and women and children of every race and every faith can join in celebration across this magnificent Mall, and why a man whose father less than sixty years ago might not have been served at a local restaurant can now stand before you to take a most sacred oath. So let us mark this day with remembrance, of who we are and how far we have traveled"

–President Barack Obama, Inagural Address

Our story is far from over. In fact it is just beginning. It is our job as Americans to rise up together to face the many challenges in the world today. We have a shared responsibility to approach these challenges with the wisdom of Abraham Lincoln, the courage of Rosa Parks, the love of Dr. Martin Luther King Jr., and the hope of President Barack Obama.

We can't erase the mistakes of the past, but together we can write the future.

Author's Note:

When President Barack Obama gave his powerful Inaugural Address, America listened to every word. What surprised and inspired me was how my second grade students listened and understood. I was moved by how connected they were. Many of my students reflected on the similarities between Barack Obama's dreams to those of Dr. Martin Luther King Jr. That beautiful, simple insight inspired this project. I hope that we can all learn something from their unbridled enthusiasm, innocence, and belief in themselves.

In his Inaugural Address, President Obama called for Americans to "pick ourselves up, dust ourselves off, and begin again the work of remaking America." I hope that this book can provide a small reply to his calling. As a public school teacher, I witness the effect of the economic crisis on our schools. A portion of the price of this book will be donated to schools in the United States. Thank you for helping bring this message to children across the nation.

-Rachael Law Schuetz

To learn more about this project and the donations made, please visit:
www.longroadtochange.com